# My Best Life

## Set In Soul

# This Journal Belongs To

*Dedicated To Every Part Of Me That Wants To Grow In The Most Positive Directions.*

# Table Of Contents

# How To Use This Journal

Are you currently living your best life? Do you honestly feel like you are doing your best in every area of your life? What do you feel like can improve on? Do you feel like there is no way out of your current situation or that you simply need the motivation to experience a better version of you? Living your best life means something different to everyone. With the everyday routine of life, it is easy to think that you may never get to live a life that you know you deserve. Sometimes it is easy to forget about the bigger picture of your life but when you focus on the positive bigger picture, you immediately become spiritually uplifted. Your best life has you smiling everyday and at peace throughout your day. It's not too late to dream up and live your best life everyday. It's not simply what kids do but what everyone does when they need change. When you begin to truly spend time with yourself and envision what it is you need, you can start working towards accepting what belongs to you and removing yourself from the people and places that do not fit into your best life. Your best life is a place where love, acceptance and respect resides. There may be some materialistic things you want and that is okay. You may want to travel or start a business or welcome in romance or a better relationship into your life. Those are all okay. So why not start living your best life? It's time to stop focusing on the negative and start believing in what will happen for yourself with just a few changes to support what belongs to you.

We recommend using this journal daily and keeping this journal close to you to remind yourself of what your best life looks like and if your actions and thoughts align with your best life. Fill in the daily prompts every morning and every night so you can start shifting your mind and spirit towards the act of living in the way you desire. There are motivational quotes throughout this journal to inspire you to create your ideal best life for yourself while enjoying where you are today. So Let's Get Started.

# How To Use This Journal

Are you currently living your best life? Do you honestly feel like you are doing your best in every area of your life? What do you feel like can improve on? Do you feel like there is no way out of your current situation or that you simply need the motivation to experience a better version of you? Living your best life means something different to everyone. With the everyday routine of life, it is easy to think that you may never get to live a life that you know you deserve. Sometimes it is easy to forget about the bigger picture of your life but when you focus on the positive bigger picture, you immediately become spiritually uplifted. Your best life has you smiling everyday and at peace throughout your day. It's not too late to dream up and live your best life everyday. It's not simply what kids do but what everyone does when they need change. When you begin to truly spend time with yourself and envision what it is you need, you can start working towards accepting what belongs to you and removing yourself from the people and places that do not fit into your best life. Your best life is a place where love, acceptance and respect resides. There may be some materialistic things you want and that is okay. You may want to travel or start a business or welcome in romance or a better relationship into your life. Those are all okay. So why not start living your best life? It's time to stop focusing on the negative and start believing in what will happen for yourself with just a few changes to support what belongs to you.

We recommend using this journal daily and keeping this journal close to you to remind yourself of what your best life looks like and if your actions and thoughts align with your best life. Fill in the daily prompts every morning and every night so you can start shifting your mind and spirit towards the act of living in the way you desire. There are motivational quotes throughout this journal to inspire you to create your ideal best life for yourself while enjoying where you are today. So Let's Get Started.

# Table Of Contents

# My Best Life:

# What Was

# *My Best Life: What Was*

I Lived Life As:

I Was Always In:

My Beliefs Were:

My Relationships Felt:

I Always Woke Up:

# *My Best Life: What Was*

I've Always Tried To:

My Home Felt:

My Health Was:

My Money:

I Always Felt Like I:

# *My Best Life: What Was*

My Limiting Beliefs Were:

My Job Was:

I Consistently Thought About:

I Kept Feeling Guilty About:

I Felt Stuck At:

# My Best Life: What Was

I Would Get Upset When:

My Thoughts Manifested:

I Knew:

When I Was Younger:

I've Experienced:

# My Best Life: What Was

I Came From:

# My Best Life: What Is

# *My Best Life: What Is*

I Love To:

I Am Passionate About:

I Work Towards:

Goals I Am Currently Working Towards Accomplishing:

Friends I Do Have:

# My Best Life: What Is

I Must Stop:

I Must Not Allow:

I Must Be Able To Allow:

I Find Satisfaction In:

I Love Spending Time:

# *My Best Life: What Is*

My Body Feels:

Dreams I Will Pursue:

I Desire:

What Makes Me Feel Bad?

What Makes Me Feel Good?

# *My Best Life: What Is*

What Makes Me Doubt?

What I Want Is:

It's Fun To:

My Work Is:

I Value:

# *My Best Life: What Is*

I Believe:

What Is Stopping Me From My Best Life?

How Much Mental Work Is Needed For Me To Feel My Best Life?

When I Think About My Best Life, It Makes Me Want To:

What Comes Easily To Me?

# My Best Life: What Is

I Wake Up At:

I Go To Bed At:

I Naturally Like:

I View Myself As:

I View People In General:

# *My Best Life: What Is*

I View The World As:

Do I Feel Like I'm Good Enough?

If No To The Above Question, Then When Do I Ever Feel Like I'm Good Enough?

I Am Moving In A Direction Towards:

Everyday I Am Choosing To Work On:

# My Best Life: What Is

The Car I Currently Drive (Answer If Applicable):

The Mindset I Currently Have:

The People I Currently Have Around Me:

The Foods I Currently Eat:

The Job I Currently Have (Answer If Applicable):

# *My Best Life: What Is*

The Business I Currently Run (If Applicable):

Currently, Everyday Feels Like:

When Something/Someone Tries To Upset Me:

My Best Life Focuses On:

I Currently Focus On:

# *My Best Life: What Is*

My Life Can Currently Improve:

Life Before Today Was:

My Future Is Looking:

Right Now I Am Changing:

How Close Am I To Living My Best Life?

# *My Best Life: What Is*

Why Is Everything I Want To Have And Feel Considered My Best Life?

If I Was Living My Best Life Now, Would I Eventually Outgrow It?

How Has My Life Been Progressing?

The Steps I Believe It Takes To Live My Best Life:

My Best Life Theme Song:

# *My Best Life: What Is*

What About My Life Now That I Do Not Want To Change?

My Current Days Look Like:

My Current Days Feels Like:

Love Feels Like:

My Relationships Are:

# *My Best Life: What Is*

My Career:

Living My Best Life Means:

The Amount Of Money I Make Annually:

# My Best Life:

# What Will Be

# *My Best Life: What Will Be*

I Prefer To Spend My Time:

I Focus On:

I Believe I Can:

Everyday I Feel:

Actions I Take Everyday Towards Living My Best Life:

# *My Best Life: What Will Be*

I Find Satisfaction In:

I Love Spending Time:

My Body Feels:

My Vacations Are:

My Vacations Feel Like:

# My Best Life: What Will Be

It's Fun To:

The People I Have Around Me:

I Would Like The People Around Me To Give:

I Would Like To Give To The People Around Me:

I Enjoy Spending My Time:

# *My Best Life: What Will Be*

I Am Always:

I Show Up In My Best Life By:

My Best Life Is Free From:

My Best Life Welcomes:

The People I Currently Know That Are Welcomed In My Best Life:

# My Best Life: What Will Be

What Comes Easily To Me?

I Wake Up At:

I Go To Bed At:

I View Myself As:

I View People In General:

# *My Best Life: What Will Be*

I View The World As:

The Foods I Enjoy Eating:

Places I Love To Go To:

I Enjoy Experiencing:

I Love Driving:

# My Best Life: What Will Be

My Business Is (Answer If Applicable):

I Am The Type Of Leader:

Everyday I Feel:

What Comes Easily To Me?

How Much Money Do I Have?

# *My Best Life: What Will Be*

Daily I Spend:

Weekly I Spend:

Monthly I Spend:

The One Thing That I Love Doing All Day:

*Living My Best Life Everyday*

# *Living My Best Life Everyday*
## *Morning Thoughts*

Date:                                          I Feel:

I Believe Today Will Be:

I Am Grateful For:

I Woke Up Repeating To Myself:

## *Nightly Thoughts*

Time:                                          I Feel:

I Would Describe Today To Be:          Today I Started/Stopped:

My Actions Towards My Best Life        Today I Ignored/Listened To:
Were:

I Invested In:                               Today's Happiest Moment:

I Spent Time With God By:                What I Did Today That I Wanted To
                                             Do:

I Showed Love Today By:_____.

# *Living My Best Life Everyday*
## *Morning Thoughts*

Date:                                    I Feel:

I Believe Today Will Be:

I Am Grateful For:

I Woke Up Repeating To Myself:

## *Nightly Thoughts*

Time:                                    I Feel:

I Would Describe Today To Be:            Today I Started/Stopped:

My Actions Towards My Best Life          Today I Ignored/Listened To:
Were:

I Invested In:                           Today's Happiest Moment:

I Spent Time With God By:                What I Did Today That I Wanted To
                                         Do:

I Showed Love Today By:_____.

# *Living My Best Life Everyday*
## *Morning Thoughts*

Date:                                I Feel:

I Believe Today Will Be:

I Am Grateful For:

I Woke Up Repeating To Myself:

## *Nightly Thoughts*

Time:                               I Feel:

| | |
|---|---|
| I Would Describe Today To Be: | Today I Started/Stopped: |
| My Actions Towards My Best Life Were: | Today I Ignored/Listened To: |
| I Invested In: | Today's Happiest Moment: |
| I Spent Time With God By: | What I Did Today That I Wanted To Do: |

I Showed Love Today By:_____.

# Everyday I Try My Best And I Am Happy With That.

# I Am Always Learning.

# *Living My Best Life Everyday*
## *Morning Thoughts*

Date:                                    I Feel:

I Believe Today Will Be:

I Am Grateful For:

I Woke Up Repeating To Myself:

## *Nightly Thoughts*

Time:                                    I Feel:

I Would Describe Today To Be:            Today I Started/Stopped:

My Actions Towards My Best Life          Today I Ignored/Listened To:
Were:

I Invested In:                           Today's Happiest Moment:

I Spent Time With God By:                What I Did Today That I Wanted To
                                         Do:

I Showed Love Today By:_____.

# Living My Best Life Everyday
## Morning Thoughts

Date:                                    I Feel:

I Believe Today Will Be:

I Am Grateful For:

I Woke Up Repeating To Myself:

# Nightly Thoughts

Time:                                    I Feel:

| | |
|---|---|
| I Would Describe Today To Be: | Today I Started/Stopped: |
| My Actions Towards My Best Life Were: | Today I Ignored/Listened To: |
| I Invested In: | Today's Happiest Moment: |
| I Spent Time With God By: | What I Did Today That I Wanted To Do: |

I Showed Love Today By:_____.

# *Living My Best Life Everyday*
## *Morning Thoughts*

Date:                                    I Feel:

I Believe Today Will Be:

I Am Grateful For:

I Woke Up Repeating To Myself:

## *Nightly Thoughts*

Time:                                    I Feel:

I Would Describe Today To Be:            Today I Started/Stopped:

My Actions Towards My Best Life          Today I Ignored/Listened To:
Were:

I Invested In:                           Today's Happiest Moment:

I Spent Time With God By:                What I Did Today That I Wanted To
                                         Do:

I Showed Love Today By:_____.

**44**

# I Look Forward To Loving....

# *Living My Best Life Everyday*
## *Morning Thoughts*

Date:                                    I Feel:

I Believe Today Will Be:

I Am Grateful For:

I Woke Up Repeating To Myself:

## *Nightly Thoughts*

Time:                                    I Feel:

I Would Describe Today To Be:          Today I Started/Stopped:

My Actions Towards My Best Life        Today I Ignored/Listened To:
Were:

I Invested In:                         Today's Happiest Moment:

I Spent Time With God By:               What I Did Today That I Wanted To
                                       Do:

I Showed Love Today By:_____.

# My Best Life Has The Best People That Are Right For Me.

I Make It A Habit To Take Chances. That's How I'm Able To Experience Things I Have Always Dreamed Of.

# *Living My Best Life Everyday*
## *Morning Thoughts*

Date:                                    I Feel:

I Believe Today Will Be:

I Am Grateful For:

I Woke Up Repeating To Myself:

## *Nightly Thoughts*

Time:                                    I Feel:

I Would Describe Today To Be:            Today I Started/Stopped:

My Actions Towards My Best Life          Today I Ignored/Listened To:
Were:

I Invested In:                           Today's Happiest Moment:

I Spent Time With God By:                What I Did Today That I Wanted To
                                         Do:

I Showed Love Today By:_____.

# *Living My Best Life Everyday*
## *Morning Thoughts*

Date:                                    I Feel:

I Believe Today Will Be:

I Am Grateful For:

I Woke Up Repeating To Myself:

# *Nightly Thoughts*

Time:                                    I Feel:

I Would Describe Today To Be:            Today I Started/Stopped:

My Actions Towards My Best Life          Today I Ignored/Listened To:
Were:

I Invested In:                           Today's Happiest Moment:

I Spent Time With God By:                What I Did Today That I Wanted To
                                         Do:

I Showed Love Today By:_____.

**50**

# It Doesn't Matter How Things Look Now, I Am Happy.

# I Am Aligned With The Life That I Want.

# Living My Best Life Everyday
## *Morning Thoughts*

Date:                                    I Feel:

I Believe Today Will Be:

I Am Grateful For:

I Woke Up Repeating To Myself:

# *Nightly Thoughts*

Time:                                    I Feel:

I Would Describe Today To Be:            Today I Started/Stopped:

My Actions Towards My Best Life          Today I Ignored/Listened To:
Were:

I Invested In:                           Today's Happiest Moment:

I Spent Time With God By:                What I Did Today That I Wanted To
                                         Do:

I Showed Love Today By:_____.

# Best Life Notes & Thoughts

# *Places I Plan To Go This Year/Next Year....*

# Living My Best Life Everyday
## Morning Thoughts

Date:                                    I Feel:

I Believe Today Will Be:

I Am Grateful For:

I Woke Up Repeating To Myself:

# Nightly Thoughts

Time:                                    I Feel:

I Would Describe Today To Be:            Today I Started/Stopped:

My Actions Towards My Best Life          Today I Ignored/Listened To:
Were:

I Invested In:                           Today's Happiest Moment:

I Spent Time With God By:                What I Did Today That I Wanted To
                                         Do:

I Showed Love Today By:_____.

# *Living My Best Life Everyday*
## *Morning Thoughts*

Date:                                    I Feel:

I Believe Today Will Be:

I Am Grateful For:

I Woke Up Repeating To Myself:

## *Nightly Thoughts*

Time:                                    I Feel:

I Would Describe Today To Be:            Today I Started/Stopped:

My Actions Towards My Best Life          Today I Ignored/Listened To:
Were:

I Invested In:                           Today's Happiest Moment:

I Spent Time With God By:                What I Did Today That I Wanted To
                                         Do:

I Showed Love Today By:_____.

# *Living My Best Life Everyday*
## *Morning Thoughts*

Date:                                      I Feel:

I Believe Today Will Be:

I Am Grateful For:

I Woke Up Repeating To Myself:

## *Nightly Thoughts*

Time:                                      I Feel:

I Would Describe Today To Be:             Today I Started/Stopped:

My Actions Towards My Best Life            Today I Ignored/Listened To:
Were:

I Invested In:                            Today's Happiest Moment:

I Spent Time With God By:                  What I Did Today That I Wanted To
                                          Do:

I Showed Love Today By:_____.

**58**

# I Always Believe Something Wonderful Is About To Happen.

# I Know I Don't Have To Be Perfect To Be Happy.

# *Living My Best Life Everyday*
## *Morning Thoughts*

Date:                                          I Feel:

I Believe Today Will Be:

I Am Grateful For:

I Woke Up Repeating To Myself:

## *Nightly Thoughts*

Time:                                          I Feel:

I Would Describe Today To Be:          Today I Started/Stopped:

My Actions Towards My Best Life         Today I Ignored/Listened To:
Were:

I Invested In:                               Today's Happiest Moment:

I Spent Time With God By:                 What I Did Today That I Wanted To
                                               Do:

I Showed Love Today By:_____.

# *This Time Next Year I Will Be Thanking God For....*

# Living My Best Life Everyday
## Morning Thoughts

Date:                              I Feel:

I Believe Today Will Be:

I Am Grateful For:

I Woke Up Repeating To Myself:

## Nightly Thoughts

Time:                              I Feel:

I Would Describe Today To Be:      Today I Started/Stopped:

My Actions Towards My Best Life    Today I Ignored/Listened To:
Were:

I Invested In:                     Today's Happiest Moment:

I Spent Time With God By:          What I Did Today That I Wanted To
                                   Do:

I Showed Love Today By:_____.

# *Living My Best Life Everyday*
## Morning Thoughts

Date:                                        I Feel:

I Believe Today Will Be:

I Am Grateful For:

I Woke Up Repeating To Myself:

## *Nightly Thoughts*

Time:                                        I Feel:

I Would Describe Today To Be:          Today I Started/Stopped:

My Actions Towards My Best Life        Today I Ignored/Listened To:
Were:

I Invested In:                           Today's Happiest Moment:

I Spent Time With God By:                What I Did Today That I Wanted To
                                         Do:

I Showed Love Today By:_____.

# Living My Best Life Everyday
## Morning Thoughts

Date:                              I Feel:

I Believe Today Will Be:

I Am Grateful For:

I Woke Up Repeating To Myself:

## Nightly Thoughts

Time:                              I Feel:

I Would Describe Today To Be:      Today I Started/Stopped:

My Actions Towards My Best Life    Today I Ignored/Listened To:
Were:

I Invested In:                     Today's Happiest Moment:

I Spent Time With God By:          What I Did Today That I Wanted To
                                   Do:

I Showed Love Today By:_____.

# Moment By Moment I Am Doing My Best.

# Whenever I Need A Pick Me Up, I Like To Listen To These Five People....

1.

2.

3.

4.

5.

# I Can Have Everything I Want. I Will Have Everything I Want.

# Best Life Notes & Thoughts

# *Living My Best Life Everyday*
## Morning Thoughts

Date:                                  I Feel:

I Believe Today Will Be:

I Am Grateful For:

I Woke Up Repeating To Myself:

## Nightly Thoughts

Time:                                   I Feel:

| | |
|---|---|
| I Would Describe Today To Be: | Today I Started/Stopped: |
| My Actions Towards My Best Life Were: | Today I Ignored/Listened To: |
| I Invested In: | Today's Happiest Moment: |
| I Spent Time With God By: | What I Did Today That I Wanted To Do: |

I Showed Love Today By:_____.

70

# It Doesn't Matter What I'm Not. All That Matters Is What I Am.

# What Does My Best Life Need Me To Step Up In?

# *Living My Best Life Everyday*
## *Morning Thoughts*

Date:                                    I Feel:

I Believe Today Will Be:

I Am Grateful For:

I Woke Up Repeating To Myself:

# *Nightly Thoughts*

Time:                                    I Feel:

I Would Describe Today To Be:          Today I Started/Stopped:

My Actions Towards My Best Life        Today I Ignored/Listened To:
Were:

I Invested In:                          Today's Happiest Moment:

I Spent Time With God By:               What I Did Today That I Wanted To
                                        Do:

I Showed Love Today By:_____.

# *Living My Best Life Everyday*
## Morning Thoughts

Date:                                    I Feel:

I Believe Today Will Be:

I Am Grateful For:

I Woke Up Repeating To Myself:

# *Nightly Thoughts*

Time:                                    I Feel:

I Would Describe Today To Be:            Today I Started/Stopped:

My Actions Towards My Best Life          Today I Ignored/Listened To:
Were:

I Invested In:                           Today's Happiest Moment:

I Spent Time With God By:                What I Did Today That I Wanted To
                                         Do:

I Showed Love Today By:_____.

# I Live A Very Passionate Life.

# *Living My Best Life Everyday*
## *Morning Thoughts*

Date:                                      I Feel:

I Believe Today Will Be:

I Am Grateful For:

I Woke Up Repeating To Myself:

## *Nightly Thoughts*

Time:                                      I Feel:

I Would Describe Today To Be:          Today I Started/Stopped:

My Actions Towards My Best Life        Today I Ignored/Listened To:
Were:

I Invested In:                         Today's Happiest Moment:

I Spent Time With God By:              What I Did Today That I Wanted To
                                       Do:

I Showed Love Today By:_____.

# Living My Best Life Everyday
## Morning Thoughts

Date:                               I Feel:

I Believe Today Will Be:

I Am Grateful For:

I Woke Up Repeating To Myself:

# Nightly Thoughts

Time:                               I Feel:

I Would Describe Today To Be:       Today I Started/Stopped:

My Actions Towards My Best Life     Today I Ignored/Listened To:
Were:

I Invested In:                      Today's Happiest Moment:

I Spent Time With God By:           What I Did Today That I Wanted To
                                    Do:

I Showed Love Today By:_____.

# Living My Best Life Everyday
## Morning Thoughts

Date:                              I Feel:

I Believe Today Will Be:

I Am Grateful For:

I Woke Up Repeating To Myself:

# Nightly Thoughts

Time:                              I Feel:

I Would Describe Today To Be:      Today I Started/Stopped:

My Actions Towards My Best Life    Today I Ignored/Listened To:
Were:

I Invested In:                     Today's Happiest Moment:

I Spent Time With God By:          What I Did Today That I Wanted To
                                   Do:

I Showed Love Today By:_____.

# *Living My Best Life Everyday*
## *Morning Thoughts*

Date:                                          I Feel:

I Believe Today Will Be:

I Am Grateful For:

I Woke Up Repeating To Myself:

## *Nightly Thoughts*

Time:                                          I Feel:

I Would Describe Today To Be:                  Today I Started/Stopped:

My Actions Towards My Best Life                 Today I Ignored/Listened To:
Were:

I Invested In:                                 Today's Happiest Moment:

I Spent Time With God By:                       What I Did Today That I Wanted To
                                               Do:

I Showed Love Today By:_____.

# What Does Living My Best Life Mean To Me?

# Who I Was Is Not Who I Am.

# *Living My Best Life Everyday*
## *Morning Thoughts*

Date:                                    I Feel:

I Believe Today Will Be:

I Am Grateful For:

I Woke Up Repeating To Myself:

## *Nightly Thoughts*

Time:                                    I Feel:

I Would Describe Today To Be:            Today I Started/Stopped:

My Actions Towards My Best Life          Today I Ignored/Listened To:
Were:

I Invested In:                           Today's Happiest Moment:

I Spent Time With God By:                What I Did Today That I Wanted To
                                         Do:

I Showed Love Today By:_____.

# Best Life Notes & Thoughts

# I Created It In The Spirit First. That's Why It Is Here.

# Living My Best Life Everyday
## Morning Thoughts

Date:                                    I Feel:

I Believe Today Will Be:

I Am Grateful For:

I Woke Up Repeating To Myself:

## Nightly Thoughts

Time:                                    I Feel:

I Would Describe Today To Be:          | Today I Started/Stopped:

My Actions Towards My Best Life        | Today I Ignored/Listened To:
Were:

I Invested In:                         | Today's Happiest Moment:

I Spent Time With God By:              | What I Did Today That I Wanted To
                                       | Do:

I Showed Love Today By:_____.

# *Living My Best Life Everyday*
## *Morning Thoughts*

Date:                              I Feel:

I Believe Today Will Be:

I Am Grateful For:

I Woke Up Repeating To Myself:

## *Nightly Thoughts*

Time:                              I Feel:

I Would Describe Today To Be:      Today I Started/Stopped:

My Actions Towards My Best Life    Today I Ignored/Listened To:
Were:

I Invested In:                     Today's Happiest Moment:

I Spent Time With God By:          What I Did Today That I Wanted To
                                   Do:

I Showed Love Today By:_____.

**86**

# Living My Best Life Everyday
## Morning Thoughts

Date:                                    I Feel:

I Believe Today Will Be:

I Am Grateful For:

I Woke Up Repeating To Myself:

# Nightly Thoughts

Time:                                    I Feel:

I Would Describe Today To Be:          Today I Started/Stopped:

My Actions Towards My Best Life        Today I Ignored/Listened To:
Were:

I Invested In:                          Today's Happiest Moment:

I Spent Time With God By:               What I Did Today That I Wanted To
                                        Do:

I Showed Love Today By:_____.

# What's Amazing About My Life Now That I Wouldn't Want To Change?

# *Best Life Notes & Thoughts*

# Living My Best Life Everyday
## Morning Thoughts

Date:                                    I Feel:

I Believe Today Will Be:

I Am Grateful For:

I Woke Up Repeating To Myself:

## Nightly Thoughts

Time:                                    I Feel:

I Would Describe Today To Be:        | Today I Started/Stopped:

My Actions Towards My Best Life      | Today I Ignored/Listened To:
Were:

I Invested In:                       | Today's Happiest Moment:

I Spent Time With God By:            | What I Did Today That I Wanted To
                                     | Do:

I Showed Love Today By:_____.

# *Living My Best Life Everyday*

## *Morning Thoughts*

Date:                                    I Feel:

I Believe Today Will Be:

I Am Grateful For:

I Woke Up Repeating To Myself:

## *Nightly Thoughts*

Time:                                    I Feel:

I Would Describe Today To Be:        Today I Started/Stopped:

My Actions Towards My Best Life      Today I Ignored/Listened To:
Were:

I Invested In:                       Today's Happiest Moment:

I Spent Time With God By:            What I Did Today That I Wanted To
                                     Do:

I Showed Love Today By:_____.

# My Life Is Dope.

# Best Life Notes & Thoughts

# Life Before Today Was....

# *Living My Best Life Everyday*
## *Morning Thoughts*

Date:                               I Feel:

I Believe Today Will Be:

I Am Grateful For:

I Woke Up Repeating To Myself:

# *Nightly Thoughts*

Time:                               I Feel:

I Would Describe Today To Be:       Today I Started/Stopped:

My Actions Towards My Best Life     Today I Ignored/Listened To:
Were:

I Invested In:                      Today's Happiest Moment:

I Spent Time With God By:           What I Did Today That I Wanted To
                                    Do:

I Showed Love Today By:_____.

# *Living My Best Life Everyday*
## *Morning Thoughts*

Date:                                    I Feel:

I Believe Today Will Be:

I Am Grateful For:

I Woke Up Repeating To Myself:

## *Nightly Thoughts*

Time:                                    I Feel:

I Would Describe Today To Be:            Today I Started/Stopped:

My Actions Towards My Best Life          Today I Ignored/Listened To:
Were:

I Invested In:                           Today's Happiest Moment:

I Spent Time With God By:                What I Did Today That I Wanted To
                                         Do:

I Showed Love Today By:_____.

**96**

# *Living My Best Life Everyday*
## *Morning Thoughts*

Date:                                          I Feel:

I Believe Today Will Be:

I Am Grateful For:

I Woke Up Repeating To Myself:

## *Nightly Thoughts*

Time:                                          I Feel:

I Would Describe Today To Be:          Today I Started/Stopped:

My Actions Towards My Best Life          Today I Ignored/Listened To:
Were:

I Invested In:                              Today's Happiest Moment:

I Spent Time With God By:                What I Did Today That I Wanted To
                                         Do:

I Showed Love Today By:_____.

# God Chose Me.

# *Living My Best Life Everyday*
## *Morning Thoughts*

Date:                                    I Feel:

I Believe Today Will Be:

I Am Grateful For:

I Woke Up Repeating To Myself:

# *Nightly Thoughts*

Time:                                    I Feel:

I Would Describe Today To Be:            Today I Started/Stopped:

My Actions Towards My Best Life          Today I Ignored/Listened To:
Were:

I Invested In:                           Today's Happiest Moment:

I Spent Time With God By:                What I Did Today That I Wanted To
                                         Do:

I Showed Love Today By:_____.

# *Living My Best Life Everyday*
## *Morning Thoughts*

Date:                                          I Feel:

I Believe Today Will Be:

I Am Grateful For:

I Woke Up Repeating To Myself:

## *Nightly Thoughts*

Time:                                          I Feel:

I Would Describe Today To Be:          Today I Started/Stopped:

My Actions Towards My Best Life       Today I Ignored/Listened To:
Were:

I Invested In:                                Today's Happiest Moment:

I Spent Time With God By:                What I Did Today That I Wanted To
                                              Do:

I Showed Love Today By:_____.

**100**

# I Have Always Dreamed....

# Some Of My Current Prayers That God Has Already Answered....

# *Living My Best Life Everyday*
## *Morning Thoughts*

Date:                                    I Feel:

I Believe Today Will Be:

I Am Grateful For:

I Woke Up Repeating To Myself:

# *Nightly Thoughts*

Time:                                    I Feel:

I Would Describe Today To Be:            Today I Started/Stopped:

My Actions Towards My Best Life          Today I Ignored/Listened To:
Were:

I Invested In:                           Today's Happiest Moment:

I Spent Time With God By:                What I Did Today That I Wanted To
                                         Do:

I Showed Love Today By:_____.

**103**

# *Living My Best Life Everyday*
## *Morning Thoughts*

Date:                                    I Feel:

I Believe Today Will Be:

I Am Grateful For:

I Woke Up Repeating To Myself:

## *Nightly Thoughts*

Time:                                    I Feel:

I Would Describe Today To Be:            Today I Started/Stopped:

My Actions Towards My Best Life          Today I Ignored/Listened To:
Were:

I Invested In:                           Today's Happiest Moment:

I Spent Time With God By:                What I Did Today That I Wanted To
                                         Do:

I Showed Love Today By:_____.

# Best Life Notes & Thoughts

# I Know That Each Day I Am Only Getting Better.

# *Living My Best Life Everyday*
## *Morning Thoughts*

Date:                                    I Feel:

I Believe Today Will Be:

I Am Grateful For:

I Woke Up Repeating To Myself:

# *Nightly Thoughts*

Time:                                    I Feel:

I Would Describe Today To Be:            Today I Started/Stopped:

My Actions Towards My Best Life          Today I Ignored/Listened To:
Were:

I Invested In:                           Today's Happiest Moment:

I Spent Time With God By:                What I Did Today That I Wanted To
                                         Do:

I Showed Love Today By:_____.

# *Living My Best Life Everyday*
## *Morning Thoughts*

Date:                                    I Feel:

I Believe Today Will Be:

I Am Grateful For:

I Woke Up Repeating To Myself:

# *Nightly Thoughts*

Time:                                    I Feel:

I Would Describe Today To Be:            Today I Started/Stopped:

My Actions Towards My Best Life          Today I Ignored/Listened To:
Were:

I Invested In:                           Today's Happiest Moment:

I Spent Time With God By:                What I Did Today That I Wanted To
                                         Do:

I Showed Love Today By:_____.

**108**

# 5 Songs That Describe
# Me Right Now....

1.



2.



3.



4.



5.

# *Living My Best Life Everyday*
## *Morning Thoughts*

Date:                                    I Feel:

I Believe Today Will Be:

I Am Grateful For:

I Woke Up Repeating To Myself:

## *Nightly Thoughts*

Time:                                    I Feel:

I Would Describe Today To Be:          Today I Started/Stopped:

My Actions Towards My Best Life        Today I Ignored/Listened To:
Were:

I Invested In:                         Today's Happiest Moment:

I Spent Time With God By:              What I Did Today That I Wanted To
                                       Do:

I Showed Love Today By:_____.

**110**

# *Living My Best Life Everyday*
## *Morning Thoughts*

Date:                                    I Feel:

I Believe Today Will Be:

I Am Grateful For:

I Woke Up Repeating To Myself:

## *Nightly Thoughts*

Time:                                    I Feel:

I Would Describe Today To Be:            Today I Started/Stopped:

My Actions Towards My Best Life          Today I Ignored/Listened To:
Were:

I Invested In:                           Today's Happiest Moment:

I Spent Time With God By:                What I Did Today That I Wanted To
                                         Do:

I Showed Love Today By:_____.

# *Living My Best Life Everyday*
## *Morning Thoughts*

Date:                                              I Feel:

I Believe Today Will Be:


I Am Grateful For:


I Woke Up Repeating To Myself:


# *Nightly Thoughts*

Time:                                              I Feel:

I Would Describe Today To Be:          Today I Started/Stopped:


My Actions Towards My Best Life        Today I Ignored/Listened To:
Were:


I Invested In:                                     Today's Happiest Moment:


I Spent Time With God By:                 What I Did Today That I Wanted To
                                                       Do:


I Showed Love Today By:_____.

# My Dreams Are Bigger Than My Fears.

# *Living My Best Life Everyday*
## *Morning Thoughts*

Date:                                    I Feel:

I Believe Today Will Be:

I Am Grateful For:

I Woke Up Repeating To Myself:

## *Nightly Thoughts*

Time:                                    I Feel:

I Would Describe Today To Be:            Today I Started/Stopped:

My Actions Towards My Best Life          Today I Ignored/Listened To:
Were:

I Invested In:                           Today's Happiest Moment:

I Spent Time With God By:                What I Did Today That I Wanted To
                                         Do:

I Showed Love Today By:_____.

**114**

# *Living My Best Life Everyday*
## *Morning Thoughts*

Date:                                    I Feel:

I Believe Today Will Be:

I Am Grateful For:

I Woke Up Repeating To Myself:

## *Nightly Thoughts*

Time:                                    I Feel:

I Would Describe Today To Be:        Today I Started/Stopped:

My Actions Towards My Best Life      Today I Ignored/Listened To:
Were:

I Invested In:                        Today's Happiest Moment:

I Spent Time With God By:             What I Did Today That I Wanted To
                                     Do:

I Showed Love Today By:_____.

# It Doesn't Matter What Looks Bad, When All I Can See Is The Good.

# I Look Forward To Winning....

# Living My Best Life Everyday

## Morning Thoughts

Date:                                    I Feel:

I Believe Today Will Be:

I Am Grateful For:

I Woke Up Repeating To Myself:

## Nightly Thoughts

Time:                                    I Feel:

I Would Describe Today To Be:            Today I Started/Stopped:

My Actions Towards My Best Life          Today I Ignored/Listened To:
Were:

I Invested In:                           Today's Happiest Moment:

I Spent Time With God By:                What I Did Today That I Wanted To
                                         Do:

I Showed Love Today By:_____.

# *Living My Best Life Everyday*
## *Morning Thoughts*

Date:                                    I Feel:

I Believe Today Will Be:

I Am Grateful For:

I Woke Up Repeating To Myself:

## *Nightly Thoughts*

Time:                                    I Feel:

I Would Describe Today To Be:        Today I Started/Stopped:

My Actions Towards My Best Life      Today I Ignored/Listened To:
Were:

I Invested In:                       Today's Happiest Moment:

I Spent Time With God By:            What I Did Today That I Wanted To
                                     Do:

I Showed Love Today By:_____.

**119**

# Best Life Notes & Thoughts

I Can Imagine Everything I Want And Then Expect God To Multiply It By 100%.

# Living My Best Life Everyday
## Morning Thoughts

Date:                                    I Feel:

I Believe Today Will Be:

I Am Grateful For:

I Woke Up Repeating To Myself:

# Nightly Thoughts

Time:                                    I Feel:

I Would Describe Today To Be:            Today I Started/Stopped:

My Actions Towards My Best Life          Today I Ignored/Listened To:
Were:

I Invested In:                           Today's Happiest Moment:

I Spent Time With God By:                What I Did Today That I Wanted To
                                         Do:

I Showed Love Today By:_____.

# Living My Best Life Everyday
## Morning Thoughts

Date:                                    I Feel:

I Believe Today Will Be:

I Am Grateful For:

I Woke Up Repeating To Myself:

## Nightly Thoughts

Time:                                    I Feel:

I Would Describe Today To Be:            Today I Started/Stopped:

My Actions Towards My Best Life          Today I Ignored/Listened To:
Were:

I Invested In:                           Today's Happiest Moment:

I Spent Time With God By:                What I Did Today That I Wanted To
                                         Do:

I Showed Love Today By:_____.

# *Bible Verses That Keep Me Encouraged....*

# *Living My Best Life Everyday*
## *Morning Thoughts*

Date:                                    I Feel:

I Believe Today Will Be:

I Am Grateful For:

I Woke Up Repeating To Myself:

## *Nightly Thoughts*

Time:                                    I Feel:

I Would Describe Today To Be:            Today I Started/Stopped:

My Actions Towards My Best Life          Today I Ignored/Listened To:
Were:

I Invested In:                           Today's Happiest Moment:

I Spent Time With God By:                What I Did Today That I Wanted To
                                         Do:

I Showed Love Today By:_____.

**125**

# *Living My Best Life Everyday*
## *Morning Thoughts*

Date:                              I Feel:

I Believe Today Will Be:

I Am Grateful For:

I Woke Up Repeating To Myself:

# *Nightly Thoughts*

Time:                              I Feel:

I Would Describe Today To Be:      Today I Started/Stopped:

My Actions Towards My Best Life    Today I Ignored/Listened To:
Were:

I Invested In:                     Today's Happiest Moment:

I Spent Time With God By:          What I Did Today That I Wanted To
                                   Do:

I Showed Love Today By:_____.

# *Living My Best Life Everyday*
## *Morning Thoughts*

Date:                                        I Feel:

I Believe Today Will Be:

I Am Grateful For:

I Woke Up Repeating To Myself:

## *Nightly Thoughts*

Time:                                        I Feel:

I Would Describe Today To Be:        Today I Started/Stopped:

My Actions Towards My Best Life      Today I Ignored/Listened To:
Were:

I Invested In:                               Today's Happiest Moment:

I Spent Time With God By:             What I Did Today That I Wanted To
                                             Do:

I Showed Love Today By:_____.

# Best Life Notes & Thoughts

# Everything I Want I Need God's Help To Get It.

# Living My Best Life Everyday
## Morning Thoughts

Date:                                    I Feel:

I Believe Today Will Be:

I Am Grateful For:

I Woke Up Repeating To Myself:

# Nightly Thoughts

Time:                                    I Feel:

I Would Describe Today To Be:            Today I Started/Stopped:

My Actions Towards My Best Life          Today I Ignored/Listened To:
Were:

I Invested In:                           Today's Happiest Moment:

I Spent Time With God By:                What I Did Today That I Wanted To
                                         Do:

I Showed Love Today By:_____.

# Living My Best Life Everyday
## Morning Thoughts

Date:                                    I Feel:

I Believe Today Will Be:

I Am Grateful For:

I Woke Up Repeating To Myself:

## Nightly Thoughts

Time:                                    I Feel:

I Would Describe Today To Be:            Today I Started/Stopped:

My Actions Towards My Best Life          Today I Ignored/Listened To:
Were:

I Invested In:                           Today's Happiest Moment:

I Spent Time With God By:                What I Did Today That I Wanted To
                                         Do:

I Showed Love Today By:_____.

# Living My Best Life Everyday
## Morning Thoughts

Date:                                    I Feel:

I Believe Today Will Be:

I Am Grateful For:

I Woke Up Repeating To Myself:

# Nightly Thoughts

Time:                                    I Feel:

I Would Describe Today To Be:            Today I Started/Stopped:

My Actions Towards My Best Life          Today I Ignored/Listened To:
Were:

I Invested In:                           Today's Happiest Moment:

I Spent Time With God By:                What I Did Today That I Wanted To
                                         Do:

I Showed Love Today By:_____.

# I Would Describe This Part Of My Life....

# *Living My Best Life Everyday*
## *Morning Thoughts*

Date:                                          I Feel:

I Believe Today Will Be:

I Am Grateful For:

I Woke Up Repeating To Myself:


# *Nightly Thoughts*

Time:                                          I Feel:

I Would Describe Today To Be:          Today I Started/Stopped:

My Actions Towards My Best Life        Today I Ignored/Listened To:
Were:

I Invested In:                                  Today's Happiest Moment:

I Spent Time With God By:                What I Did Today That I Wanted To
                                               Do:

I Showed Love Today By:_____.

**134**

# Living My Best Life Everyday
## Morning Thoughts

Date:                                    I Feel:

I Believe Today Will Be:

I Am Grateful For:

I Woke Up Repeating To Myself:

## Nightly Thoughts

Time:                                    I Feel:

I Would Describe Today To Be:            Today I Started/Stopped:

My Actions Towards My Best Life          Today I Ignored/Listened To:
Were:

I Invested In:                           Today's Happiest Moment:

I Spent Time With God By:                What I Did Today That I Wanted To
                                         Do:

I Showed Love Today By:_____.

# Living My Best Life Everyday
## Morning Thoughts

Date:                                    I Feel:

I Believe Today Will Be:

I Am Grateful For:

I Woke Up Repeating To Myself:

# Nightly Thoughts

Time:                                    I Feel:

I Would Describe Today To Be:            Today I Started/Stopped:

My Actions Towards My Best Life          Today I Ignored/Listened To:
Were:

I Invested In:                           Today's Happiest Moment:

I Spent Time With God By:                What I Did Today That I Wanted To
                                         Do:

I Showed Love Today By:_____.

136

# Best Life Notes & Thoughts

# *What Will My New Routine Look Like As I Start To Live My Best Life....*

# Living My Best Life Everyday
## Morning Thoughts

Date:                                    I Feel:

I Believe Today Will Be:

I Am Grateful For:

I Woke Up Repeating To Myself:

# Nightly Thoughts

Time:                                    I Feel:

I Would Describe Today To Be:            Today I Started/Stopped:

My Actions Towards My Best Life          Today I Ignored/Listened To:
Were:

I Invested In:                           Today's Happiest Moment:

I Spent Time With God By:                What I Did Today That I Wanted To
                                         Do:

I Showed Love Today By:_____.

# It Doesn't Matter Who Likes Me If I Like Me.

# Living My Best Life Everyday
## Morning Thoughts

Date:                                    I Feel:

I Believe Today Will Be:

I Am Grateful For:

I Woke Up Repeating To Myself:

## Nightly Thoughts

Time:                                    I Feel:

I Would Describe Today To Be:            Today I Started/Stopped:

My Actions Towards My Best Life          Today I Ignored/Listened To:
Were:

I Invested In:                           Today's Happiest Moment:

I Spent Time With God By:                What I Did Today That I Wanted To
                                         Do:

I Showed Love Today By:_____.

# *Living My Best Life Everyday*
## *Morning Thoughts*

Date:                                    I Feel:

I Believe Today Will Be:

I Am Grateful For:

I Woke Up Repeating To Myself:

# *Nightly Thoughts*

Time:                                    I Feel:

I Would Describe Today To Be:        Today I Started/Stopped:

My Actions Towards My Best Life      Today I Ignored/Listened To:
Were:

I Invested In:                       Today's Happiest Moment:

I Spent Time With God By:            What I Did Today That I Wanted To
                                     Do:

I Showed Love Today By:_____.

**142**

# It's Okay For Me To Create What I Want To See In My Life.

# I Ignore Everyone Who Ridicules My Dreams.

# Living My Best Life Everyday
## Morning Thoughts

Date:                              I Feel:

I Believe Today Will Be:

I Am Grateful For:

I Woke Up Repeating To Myself:

## Nightly Thoughts

Time:                              I Feel:

I Would Describe Today To Be:      Today I Started/Stopped:

My Actions Towards My Best Life    Today I Ignored/Listened To:
Were:

I Invested In:                     Today's Happiest Moment:

I Spent Time With God By:          What I Did Today That I Wanted To
                                   Do:

I Showed Love Today By:_____.

# *Living My Best Life Everyday*
## *Morning Thoughts*

Date:                                    I Feel:

I Believe Today Will Be:

I Am Grateful For:

I Woke Up Repeating To Myself:

# *Nightly Thoughts*

Time:                                    I Feel:

I Would Describe Today To Be:        Today I Started/Stopped:

My Actions Towards My Best Life       Today I Ignored/Listened To:
Were:

I Invested In:                       Today's Happiest Moment:

I Spent Time With God By:             What I Did Today That I Wanted To
                                     Do:

I Showed Love Today By:_____.

**146**

# Best Life Notes & Thoughts

# Living My Best Life Everyday
## <u>Morning Thoughts</u>

Date:                                    I Feel:

I Believe Today Will Be:

I Am Grateful For:

I Woke Up Repeating To Myself:

# <u>Nightly Thoughts</u>

Time:                                    I Feel:

I Would Describe Today To Be:        Today I Started/Stopped:

My Actions Towards My Best Life      Today I Ignored/Listened To:
Were:

I Invested In:                       Today's Happiest Moment:

I Spent Time With God By:            What I Did Today That I Wanted To
                                     Do:

I Showed Love Today By:_____.

**148**

# Living My Best Life Everyday
## <u>Morning Thoughts</u>

Date:                                    I Feel:

I Believe Today Will Be:

I Am Grateful For:

I Woke Up Repeating To Myself:

# <u>Nightly Thoughts</u>

Time:                                    I Feel:

I Would Describe Today To Be:         | Today I Started/Stopped:

My Actions Towards My Best Life       | Today I Ignored/Listened To:
Were:

I Invested In:                        | Today's Happiest Moment:

I Spent Time With God By:             | What I Did Today That I Wanted To
                                      | Do:

I Showed Love Today By:_____.

# The Money I Am Making In My Best Life Is Able To Purchase/Pay For....

# I Don't Care If I'm The Only One Who Believes What I Believe.

# *Living My Best Life Everyday*
## *Morning Thoughts*

Date:                                              I Feel:

I Believe Today Will Be:

I Am Grateful For:

I Woke Up Repeating To Myself:

## *Nightly Thoughts*

Time:                                              I Feel:

I Would Describe Today To Be:          Today I Started/Stopped:

My Actions Towards My Best Life         Today I Ignored/Listened To:
Were:

I Invested In:                                     Today's Happiest Moment:

I Spent Time With God By:                  What I Did Today That I Wanted To
                                                        Do:

I Showed Love Today By:_____.

**152**

# *Living My Best Life Everyday*
## *Morning Thoughts*

Date:                                    I Feel:

I Believe Today Will Be:

I Am Grateful For:

I Woke Up Repeating To Myself:

## *Nightly Thoughts*

Time:                                    I Feel:

I Would Describe Today To Be:            Today I Started/Stopped:

My Actions Towards My Best Life          Today I Ignored/Listened To:
Were:

I Invested In:                           Today's Happiest Moment:

I Spent Time With God By:                What I Did Today That I Wanted To
                                         Do:

I Showed Love Today By:_____.

# Best Life Notes & Thoughts

# In My Best Life, I Look....

# *Living My Best Life Everyday*
## <u>*Morning Thoughts*</u>

Date:                                    I Feel:

I Believe Today Will Be:

I Am Grateful For:

I Woke Up Repeating To Myself:

# <u>*Nightly Thoughts*</u>

Time:                                    I Feel:

I Would Describe Today To Be:          Today I Started/Stopped:

My Actions Towards My Best Life        Today I Ignored/Listened To:
Were:

I Invested In:                         Today's Happiest Moment:

I Spent Time With God By:               What I Did Today That I Wanted To
                                        Do:

I Showed Love Today By:_____.

# Best Life Notes & Thoughts

# Living My Best Life Everyday
## Morning Thoughts

Date:                                    I Feel:

I Believe Today Will Be:

I Am Grateful For:

I Woke Up Repeating To Myself:

# Nightly Thoughts

Time:                                    I Feel:

I Would Describe Today To Be:          Today I Started/Stopped:

My Actions Towards My Best Life        Today I Ignored/Listened To:
Were:

I Invested In:                         Today's Happiest Moment:

I Spent Time With God By:              What I Did Today That I Wanted To
                                       Do:

I Showed Love Today By:_____.

# *Living My Best Life Everyday*

## *Morning Thoughts*

Date:                                    I Feel:

I Believe Today Will Be:

I Am Grateful For:

I Woke Up Repeating To Myself:

## *Nightly Thoughts*

Time:                                    I Feel:

I Would Describe Today To Be:            Today I Started/Stopped:

My Actions Towards My Best Life          Today I Ignored/Listened To:
Were:

I Invested In:                           Today's Happiest Moment:

I Spent Time With God By:                What I Did Today That I Wanted To
                                         Do:

I Showed Love Today By:_____.

**159**

# God Has A Plan For Me.

# It's Never Too Late To....

# Living My Best Life Everyday
## Morning Thoughts

Date:                                    I Feel:

I Believe Today Will Be:

I Am Grateful For:

I Woke Up Repeating To Myself:

# Nightly Thoughts

Time:                                    I Feel:

I Would Describe Today To Be:         Today I Started/Stopped:

My Actions Towards My Best Life       Today I Ignored/Listened To:
Were:

I Invested In:                        Today's Happiest Moment:

I Spent Time With God By:             What I Did Today That I Wanted To
                                      Do:

I Showed Love Today By:_____.

**162**

# Living My Best Life Everyday
## Morning Thoughts

Date:                                    I Feel:

I Believe Today Will Be:

I Am Grateful For:

I Woke Up Repeating To Myself:

## Nightly Thoughts

Time:                                    I Feel:

I Would Describe Today To Be:            Today I Started/Stopped:

My Actions Towards My Best Life          Today I Ignored/Listened To:
Were:

I Invested In:                           Today's Happiest Moment:

I Spent Time With God By:                What I Did Today That I Wanted To
                                         Do:

I Showed Love Today By:_____.

# *Living My Best Life Everyday*
## *Morning Thoughts*

Date:                                    I Feel:

I Believe Today Will Be:

I Am Grateful For:

I Woke Up Repeating To Myself:

## *Nightly Thoughts*

Time:                                    I Feel:

I Would Describe Today To Be:            Today I Started/Stopped:

My Actions Towards My Best Life          Today I Ignored/Listened To:
Were:

I Invested In:                           Today's Happiest Moment:

I Spent Time With God By:                What I Did Today That I Wanted To
                                         Do:

I Showed Love Today By:_____.

**164**

# I Choose To Live In My Truth Than To Live In Their Lie.

# Moving Forward, Everyday Is A Great Day.

# *Living My Best Life Everyday*
## *Morning Thoughts*

Date:                                    I Feel:

I Believe Today Will Be:

I Am Grateful For:

I Woke Up Repeating To Myself:

## *Nightly Thoughts*

Time:                                    I Feel:

I Would Describe Today To Be:            Today I Started/Stopped:

My Actions Towards My Best Life          Today I Ignored/Listened To:
Were:

I Invested In:                           Today's Happiest Moment:

I Spent Time With God By:                What I Did Today That I Wanted To
                                         Do:

I Showed Love Today By:_____.

# *Living My Best Life Everyday*
## *Morning Thoughts*

Date:                                          I Feel:

I Believe Today Will Be:

I Am Grateful For:

I Woke Up Repeating To Myself:

## *Nightly Thoughts*

Time:                                          I Feel:

I Would Describe Today To Be:          Today I Started/Stopped:

My Actions Towards My Best Life        Today I Ignored/Listened To:
Were:

I Invested In:                                  Today's Happiest Moment:

I Spent Time With God By:                 What I Did Today That I Wanted To
                                               Do:

I Showed Love Today By:_____.

# Living My Best Life Everyday
## Morning Thoughts

Date:                                          I Feel:

I Believe Today Will Be:

I Am Grateful For:

I Woke Up Repeating To Myself:

# Nightly Thoughts

Time:                                          I Feel:

I Would Describe Today To Be:          Today I Started/Stopped:

My Actions Towards My Best Life        Today I Ignored/Listened To:
Were:

I Invested In:                                 Today's Happiest Moment:

I Spent Time With God By:                What I Did Today That I Wanted To
                                              Do:

I Showed Love Today By:_____.

# Best Life Notes & Thoughts

# I Have The Courage To Ask And Believe In Something Better.

# Living My Best Life Everyday
## Morning Thoughts

Date:                                        I Feel:

I Believe Today Will Be:

I Am Grateful For:

I Woke Up Repeating To Myself:

## Nightly Thoughts

Time:                                        I Feel:

I Would Describe Today To Be:          Today I Started/Stopped:

My Actions Towards My Best Life        Today I Ignored/Listened To:
Were:

I Invested In:                            Today's Happiest Moment:

I Spent Time With God By:                 What I Did Today That I Wanted To
                                          Do:

I Showed Love Today By:_____.

172

# I Am Creating And Living The Life That I Want.

# *Living My Best Life Everyday*
## *Morning Thoughts*

Date:                                    I Feel:

I Believe Today Will Be:

I Am Grateful For:

I Woke Up Repeating To Myself:

# *Nightly Thoughts*

Time:                                    I Feel:

I Would Describe Today To Be:        | Today I Started/Stopped:

My Actions Towards My Best Life      | Today I Ignored/Listened To:
Were:

I Invested In:                       | Today's Happiest Moment:

I Spent Time With God By:            | What I Did Today That I Wanted To
                                     | Do:

I Showed Love Today By:_____.

# *Living My Best Life Everyday*
## *Morning Thoughts*

Date:                                          I Feel:

I Believe Today Will Be:

I Am Grateful For:

I Woke Up Repeating To Myself:

## *Nightly Thoughts*

Time:                                          I Feel:

I Would Describe Today To Be:          Today I Started/Stopped:

My Actions Towards My Best Life        Today I Ignored/Listened To:
Were:

I Invested In:                                 Today's Happiest Moment:

I Spent Time With God By:                 What I Did Today That I Wanted To
                                               Do:

I Showed Love Today By:_____.

# *Living My Best Life Everyday*
## *Morning Thoughts*

Date:                                    I Feel:

I Believe Today Will Be:

I Am Grateful For:

I Woke Up Repeating To Myself:

## *Nightly Thoughts*

Time:                                    I Feel:

I Would Describe Today To Be:         Today I Started/Stopped:

My Actions Towards My Best Life       Today I Ignored/Listened To:
Were:

I Invested In:                        Today's Happiest Moment:

I Spent Time With God By:             What I Did Today That I Wanted To
                                      Do:

I Showed Love Today By:_____.

**176**

# There Is No Limit To What I Can Have.

# I Will Allow No One To Make Me Feel Guilty About My Blessings.

# Living My Best Life Everyday
## Morning Thoughts

Date:                                    I Feel:

I Believe Today Will Be:

I Am Grateful For:

I Woke Up Repeating To Myself:

# Nightly Thoughts

Time:                                    I Feel:

I Would Describe Today To Be:            Today I Started/Stopped:

My Actions Towards My Best Life          Today I Ignored/Listened To:
Were:

I Invested In:                           Today's Happiest Moment:

I Spent Time With God By:                What I Did Today That I Wanted To
                                         Do:

I Showed Love Today By:_____.

# Living My Best Life Everyday

## Morning Thoughts

Date:                                    I Feel:

I Believe Today Will Be:

I Am Grateful For:

I Woke Up Repeating To Myself:

## Nightly Thoughts

Time:                                    I Feel:

I Would Describe Today To Be:            Today I Started/Stopped:

My Actions Towards My Best Life          Today I Ignored/Listened To:
Were:

I Invested In:                           Today's Happiest Moment:

I Spent Time With God By:                What I Did Today That I Wanted To
                                         Do:

I Showed Love Today By:_____.

# I Love Where I Am Right Now.

# I Am Living My Best Life.

# Living My Best Life Everyday
## Morning Thoughts

Date:                                    I Feel:

I Believe Today Will Be:

I Am Grateful For:

I Woke Up Repeating To Myself:

# Nightly Thoughts

Time:                                    I Feel:

I Would Describe Today To Be:            Today I Started/Stopped:

My Actions Towards My Best Life          Today I Ignored/Listened To:
Were:

I Invested In:                           Today's Happiest Moment:

I Spent Time With God By:                What I Did Today That I Wanted To
                                         Do:

I Showed Love Today By:_____.

# *Living My Best Life Everyday*
## *Morning Thoughts*

Date:                                    I Feel:

I Believe Today Will Be:

I Am Grateful For:

I Woke Up Repeating To Myself:

## *Nightly Thoughts*

Time:                                    I Feel:

I Would Describe Today To Be:            Today I Started/Stopped:

My Actions Towards My Best Life          Today I Ignored/Listened To:
Were:

I Invested In:                           Today's Happiest Moment:

I Spent Time With God By:                What I Did Today That I Wanted To
                                         Do:

I Showed Love Today By:_____.

**184**

# Living My Best Life Everyday
## Morning Thoughts

Date:                                    I Feel:

I Believe Today Will Be:

I Am Grateful For:

I Woke Up Repeating To Myself:

## Nightly Thoughts

Time:                                    I Feel:

I Would Describe Today To Be:            Today I Started/Stopped:

My Actions Towards My Best Life          Today I Ignored/Listened To:
Were:

I Invested In:                           Today's Happiest Moment:

I Spent Time With God By:                What I Did Today That I Wanted To
                                         Do:

I Showed Love Today By:_____.

# *Everyday I Am Choosing To Feel....*

# Best Life Notes & Thoughts

# *Living My Best Life Everyday*
## *Morning Thoughts*

Date:                                    I Feel:

I Believe Today Will Be:

I Am Grateful For:

I Woke Up Repeating To Myself:

# *Nightly Thoughts*

Time:                                    I Feel:

I Would Describe Today To Be:            Today I Started/Stopped:

My Actions Towards My Best Life          Today I Ignored/Listened To:
Were:

I Invested In:                           Today's Happiest Moment:

I Spent Time With God By:                What I Did Today That I Wanted To
                                         Do:

I Showed Love Today By:_____.

# Living My Best Life Everyday
## Morning Thoughts

Date:                                    I Feel:

I Believe Today Will Be:

I Am Grateful For:

I Woke Up Repeating To Myself:

# Nightly Thoughts

Time:                                    I Feel:

I Would Describe Today To Be:            Today I Started/Stopped:

My Actions Towards My Best Life          Today I Ignored/Listened To:
Were:

I Invested In:                           Today's Happiest Moment:

I Spent Time With God By:                What I Did Today That I Wanted To
                                         Do:

I Showed Love Today By:_____.

# *Living My Best Life Everyday*
## *Morning Thoughts*

Date:                                    I Feel:

I Believe Today Will Be:

I Am Grateful For:

I Woke Up Repeating To Myself:

# *Nightly Thoughts*

Time:                                    I Feel:

I Would Describe Today To Be:            Today I Started/Stopped:

My Actions Towards My Best Life          Today I Ignored/Listened To:
Were:

I Invested In:                           Today's Happiest Moment:

I Spent Time With God By:                What I Did Today That I Wanted To
                                         Do:

I Showed Love Today By:_____.

**190**

# I Will Never Give Up On God. I Will Never Give Up On Myself.

# I Have Been Meditating On....

# *Living My Best Life Everyday*

## *Morning Thoughts*

Date:                                    I Feel:

I Believe Today Will Be:

I Am Grateful For:

I Woke Up Repeating To Myself:

## *Nightly Thoughts*

Time:                                    I Feel:

I Would Describe Today To Be:            Today I Started/Stopped:

My Actions Towards My Best Life          Today I Ignored/Listened To:
Were:

I Invested In:                           Today's Happiest Moment:

I Spent Time With God By:                What I Did Today That I Wanted To
                                         Do:

I Showed Love Today By:_____.

# *Living My Best Life Everyday*
## *Morning Thoughts*

Date:                                    I Feel:

I Believe Today Will Be:

I Am Grateful For:

I Woke Up Repeating To Myself:

# *Nightly Thoughts*

Time:                                    I Feel:

I Would Describe Today To Be:          Today I Started/Stopped:

My Actions Towards My Best Life        Today I Ignored/Listened To:
Were:

I Invested In:                         Today's Happiest Moment:

I Spent Time With God By:              What I Did Today That I Wanted To
                                       Do:

I Showed Love Today By:_____.

**194**

# Living My Best Life Everyday
## Morning Thoughts

Date:                                    I Feel:

I Believe Today Will Be:

I Am Grateful For:

I Woke Up Repeating To Myself:

# Nightly Thoughts

Time:                                    I Feel:

I Would Describe Today To Be:          Today I Started/Stopped:

My Actions Towards My Best Life        Today I Ignored/Listened To:
Were:

I Invested In:                          Today's Happiest Moment:

I Spent Time With God By:               What I Did Today That I Wanted To
                                        Do:

I Showed Love Today By:_____.

# Best Life Notes & Thoughts

# I Am Feeling Confident About....

# *Living My Best Life Everyday*
## *Morning Thoughts*

Date:                                    I Feel:

I Believe Today Will Be:

I Am Grateful For:

I Woke Up Repeating To Myself:

# *Nightly Thoughts*

Time:                                    I Feel:

I Would Describe Today To Be:            Today I Started/Stopped:

My Actions Towards My Best Life          Today I Ignored/Listened To:
Were:

I Invested In:                           Today's Happiest Moment:

I Spent Time With God By:                What I Did Today That I Wanted To
                                         Do:

I Showed Love Today By:_____.

**198**

# In This New Life, I'm Just Vibrating Higher.

# I Stayed True To God And He Made All My Dreams Come True.

# Best Life Notes & Thoughts

# *Living My Best Life Everyday*
## *Morning Thoughts*

Date:                                    I Feel:

I Believe Today Will Be:

I Am Grateful For:

I Woke Up Repeating To Myself:

## *Nightly Thoughts*

Time:                                    I Feel:

I Would Describe Today To Be:          Today I Started/Stopped:

My Actions Towards My Best Life        Today I Ignored/Listened To:
Were:

I Invested In:                         Today's Happiest Moment:

I Spent Time With God By:              What I Did Today That I Wanted To
                                       Do:

I Showed Love Today By:_____.

# *Living My Best Life Everyday*
## <u>*Morning Thoughts*</u>

Date:                                    I Feel:

I Believe Today Will Be:

I Am Grateful For:

I Woke Up Repeating To Myself:


# <u>*Nightly Thoughts*</u>

Time:                                    I Feel:

I Would Describe Today To Be:            Today I Started/Stopped:

My Actions Towards My Best Life          Today I Ignored/Listened To:
Were:

I Invested In:                           Today's Happiest Moment:

I Spent Time With God By:                What I Did Today That I Wanted To
                                         Do:

I Showed Love Today By:_____.

# *Living My Best Life Everyday*
## *Morning Thoughts*

Date:                                    I Feel:

I Believe Today Will Be:

I Am Grateful For:

I Woke Up Repeating To Myself:

# *Nightly Thoughts*

Time:                                    I Feel:

I Would Describe Today To Be:            Today I Started/Stopped:

My Actions Towards My Best Life          Today I Ignored/Listened To:
Were:

I Invested In:                           Today's Happiest Moment:

I Spent Time With God By:                What I Did Today That I Wanted To
                                         Do:

I Showed Love Today By:_____.

# I Am Unapologetic About....

# My Blessings Bless Others.

# Living My Best Life Everyday
## <u>Morning Thoughts</u>

Date:                                    I Feel:

I Believe Today Will Be:

I Am Grateful For:

I Woke Up Repeating To Myself:

## <u>Nightly Thoughts</u>

Time:                                    I Feel:

I Would Describe Today To Be:          | Today I Started/Stopped:

My Actions Towards My Best Life        | Today I Ignored/Listened To:
Were:

I Invested In:                         | Today's Happiest Moment:

I Spent Time With God By:              | What I Did Today That I Wanted To
                                       | Do:

I Showed Love Today By:_____.

# Best Life Notes & Thoughts

# Living My Best Life Everyday
## Morning Thoughts

Date:                                I Feel:

I Believe Today Will Be:

I Am Grateful For:

I Woke Up Repeating To Myself:

## Nightly Thoughts

Time:                                I Feel:

I Would Describe Today To Be:        Today I Started/Stopped:

My Actions Towards My Best Life      Today I Ignored/Listened To:
Were:

I Invested In:                       Today's Happiest Moment:

I Spent Time With God By:            What I Did Today That I Wanted To
                                     Do:

I Showed Love Today By:_____.

# Dear God, You Are So Good To Me.

# I Prayed For It.

# *Living My Best Life Everyday*
## *Morning Thoughts*

Date:                                    I Feel:

I Believe Today Will Be:

I Am Grateful For:

I Woke Up Repeating To Myself:

# *Nightly Thoughts*

Time:                                    I Feel:

I Would Describe Today To Be:            Today I Started/Stopped:

My Actions Towards My Best Life          Today I Ignored/Listened To:
Were:

I Invested In:                           Today's Happiest Moment:

I Spent Time With God By:                What I Did Today That I Wanted To
                                         Do:

I Showed Love Today By:_____.

212

# *Living My Best Life Everyday*
## *Morning Thoughts*

Date:                              I Feel:

I Believe Today Will Be:

I Am Grateful For:

I Woke Up Repeating To Myself:

## *Nightly Thoughts*

Time:                              I Feel:

I Would Describe Today To Be:      Today I Started/Stopped:

My Actions Towards My Best Life    Today I Ignored/Listened To:
Were:

I Invested In:                     Today's Happiest Moment:

I Spent Time With God By:          What I Did Today That I Wanted To
                                   Do:

I Showed Love Today By:_____.

# Best Life Notes & Thoughts

# I Choose To Invest In Me.

# *Living My Best Life Everyday*
## *Morning Thoughts*

Date:                                    I Feel:

I Believe Today Will Be:

I Am Grateful For:

I Woke Up Repeating To Myself:

# *Nightly Thoughts*

Time:                                    I Feel:

I Would Describe Today To Be:            Today I Started/Stopped:

My Actions Towards My Best Life          Today I Ignored/Listened To:
Were:

I Invested In:                           Today's Happiest Moment:

I Spent Time With God By:                What I Did Today That I Wanted To
                                         Do:

I Showed Love Today By:_____.

**216**

# Living My Best Life Everyday
## Morning Thoughts

Date:                               I Feel:

I Believe Today Will Be:

I Am Grateful For:

I Woke Up Repeating To Myself:

## Nightly Thoughts

Time:                               I Feel:

I Would Describe Today To Be:       Today I Started/Stopped:

My Actions Towards My Best Life     Today I Ignored/Listened To:
Were:

I Invested In:                      Today's Happiest Moment:

I Spent Time With God By:           What I Did Today That I Wanted To
                                    Do:

I Showed Love Today By:_____.

# I Keep Going Because....

# *Living My Best Life Everyday*
## <u>*Morning Thoughts*</u>

Date:                                    I Feel:

I Believe Today Will Be:

I Am Grateful For:

I Woke Up Repeating To Myself:

# <u>*Nightly Thoughts*</u>

Time:                                    I Feel:

I Would Describe Today To Be:        | Today I Started/Stopped:

My Actions Towards My Best Life      | Today I Ignored/Listened To:
Were:

I Invested In:                       | Today's Happiest Moment:

I Spent Time With God By:            | What I Did Today That I Wanted To
                                     | Do:

I Showed Love Today By:_____.

# I Appreciate My Journey As It Prepares Me For My Destination.

I Look Back At My Old Life And Say Thank You For Helping Me To Create A Better Life.

# Living My Best Life Everyday
## Morning Thoughts

Date:                                    I Feel:

I Believe Today Will Be:

I Am Grateful For:

I Woke Up Repeating To Myself:

## Nightly Thoughts

Time:                                    I Feel:

I Would Describe Today To Be:           | Today I Started/Stopped:

My Actions Towards My Best Life         | Today I Ignored/Listened To:
Were:

I Invested In:                          | Today's Happiest Moment:

I Spent Time With God By:                | What I Did Today That I Wanted To
                                          Do:

I Showed Love Today By:_____.

**222**

# Living My Best Life Everyday
## <u>Morning Thoughts</u>

Date:                                    I Feel:

I Believe Today Will Be:

I Am Grateful For:

I Woke Up Repeating To Myself:

# <u>Nightly Thoughts</u>

Time:                                    I Feel:

I Would Describe Today To Be:            Today I Started/Stopped:

My Actions Towards My Best Life          Today I Ignored/Listened To:
Were:

I Invested In:                           Today's Happiest Moment:

I Spent Time With God By:                What I Did Today That I Wanted To
                                         Do:

I Showed Love Today By:_____.

# Other People Who Would Benefit From Me Living My Best Life....

# Best Life Notes & Thoughts

# Living My Best Life Everyday
## Morning Thoughts

Date:                                    I Feel:

I Believe Today Will Be:

I Am Grateful For:

I Woke Up Repeating To Myself:

# Nightly Thoughts

Time:                                    I Feel:

I Would Describe Today To Be:            Today I Started/Stopped:

My Actions Towards My Best Life          Today I Ignored/Listened To:
Were:

I Invested In:                           Today's Happiest Moment:

I Spent Time With God By:                What I Did Today That I Wanted To
                                         Do:

I Showed Love Today By:_____.

**226**

# Living My Best Life Everyday
## Morning Thoughts

Date:                                  I Feel:

I Believe Today Will Be:

I Am Grateful For:

I Woke Up Repeating To Myself:

## Nightly Thoughts

Time:                                  I Feel:

I Would Describe Today To Be:          Today I Started/Stopped:

My Actions Towards My Best Life        Today I Ignored/Listened To:
Were:

I Invested In:                         Today's Happiest Moment:

I Spent Time With God By:               What I Did Today That I Wanted To
                                       Do:

I Showed Love Today By:_____.

# *Living My Best Life Everyday*
## *Morning Thoughts*

Date:                                    I Feel:

I Believe Today Will Be:

I Am Grateful For:

I Woke Up Repeating To Myself:

# *Nightly Thoughts*

Time:                                    I Feel:

I Would Describe Today To Be:            Today I Started/Stopped:

My Actions Towards My Best Life          Today I Ignored/Listened To:
Were:

I Invested In:                           Today's Happiest Moment:

I Spent Time With God By:                What I Did Today That I Wanted To
                                         Do:

I Showed Love Today By:_____.

**228**

# Even When Things Don't Look Like They Are Working Out, They Always Do.

# Best Life Notes & Thoughts

# *Living My Best Life Everyday*
## *Morning Thoughts*

Date:                                   I Feel:

I Believe Today Will Be:

I Am Grateful For:

I Woke Up Repeating To Myself:

# *Nightly Thoughts*

Time:                                   I Feel:

I Would Describe Today To Be:          Today I Started/Stopped:

My Actions Towards My Best Life        Today I Ignored/Listened To:
Were:

I Invested In:                         Today's Happiest Moment:

I Spent Time With God By:              What I Did Today That I Wanted To
                                       Do:

I Showed Love Today By:_____.

# Living My Best Life Everyday
## Morning Thoughts

Date:                                    I Feel:

I Believe Today Will Be:

I Am Grateful For:

I Woke Up Repeating To Myself:

# Nightly Thoughts

Time:                                    I Feel:

I Would Describe Today To Be:            Today I Started/Stopped:

My Actions Towards My Best Life          Today I Ignored/Listened To:
Were:

I Invested In:                           Today's Happiest Moment:

I Spent Time With God By:                What I Did Today That I Wanted To
                                         Do:

I Showed Love Today By:_____.

**232**

# Living My Best Life Everyday
## Morning Thoughts

Date:                                    I Feel:

I Believe Today Will Be:

I Am Grateful For:

I Woke Up Repeating To Myself:

# Nightly Thoughts

Time:                                    I Feel:

I Would Describe Today To Be:            Today I Started/Stopped:

My Actions Towards My Best Life          Today I Ignored/Listened To:
Were:

I Invested In:                           Today's Happiest Moment:

I Spent Time With God By:                What I Did Today That I Wanted To
                                         Do:

I Showed Love Today By:_____.

# *Living My Best Life Everyday*
## *Morning Thoughts*

Date:                                    I Feel:

I Believe Today Will Be:

I Am Grateful For:

I Woke Up Repeating To Myself:

## *Nightly Thoughts*

Time:                                    I Feel:

I Would Describe Today To Be:            Today I Started/Stopped:

My Actions Towards My Best Life          Today I Ignored/Listened To:
Were:

I Invested In:                           Today's Happiest Moment:

I Spent Time With God By:                What I Did Today That I Wanted To
                                         Do:

I Showed Love Today By:_____.

# I Saw It Before It Even Showed Up.

# My Best Life Is Created And Operated With Love.

# Overdosing On Faith.

# Best Life Notes & Thoughts

# *Living My Best Life Everyday*
## <u>Morning Thoughts</u>

Date:                                    I Feel:

I Believe Today Will Be:

I Am Grateful For:

I Woke Up Repeating To Myself:

## <u>Nightly Thoughts</u>

Time:                                    I Feel:

I Would Describe Today To Be:            Today I Started/Stopped:

My Actions Towards My Best Life          Today I Ignored/Listened To:
Were:

I Invested In:                           Today's Happiest Moment:

I Spent Time With God By:                What I Did Today That I Wanted To
                                         Do:

I Showed Love Today By:_____.

# Living My Truth Means....

# Best Life Notes & Thoughts

# *Living My Best Life Everyday*
## *Morning Thoughts*

Date:                                        I Feel:

I Believe Today Will Be:

I Am Grateful For:

I Woke Up Repeating To Myself:

# *Nightly Thoughts*

Time:                                        I Feel:

I Would Describe Today To Be:        Today I Started/Stopped:

My Actions Towards My Best Life      Today I Ignored/Listened To:
Were:

I Invested In:                               Today's Happiest Moment:

I Spent Time With God By:               What I Did Today That I Wanted To
                                             Do:

I Showed Love Today By:_____.

# *Living My Best Life Everyday*
## <u>Morning Thoughts</u>

Date:                                    I Feel:

I Believe Today Will Be:

I Am Grateful For:

I Woke Up Repeating To Myself:

# <u>Nightly Thoughts</u>

Time:                                    I Feel:

| | |
|---|---|
| I Would Describe Today To Be: | Today I Started/Stopped: |
| My Actions Towards My Best Life Were: | Today I Ignored/Listened To: |
| I Invested In: | Today's Happiest Moment: |
| I Spent Time With God By: | What I Did Today That I Wanted To Do: |

I Showed Love Today By:_____.

# *Living My Best Life Everyday*
## <u>Morning Thoughts</u>

Date:                                   I Feel:

I Believe Today Will Be:

I Am Grateful For:

I Woke Up Repeating To Myself:

# *Nightly Thoughts*

Time:                                   I Feel:

I Would Describe Today To Be:          Today I Started/Stopped:

My Actions Towards My Best Life        Today I Ignored/Listened To:
Were:

I Invested In:                         Today's Happiest Moment:

I Spent Time With God By:              What I Did Today That I Wanted To
                                       Do:

I Showed Love Today By:_____.

# There Is So Much In My Life To Celebrate.

# Best Life Notes & Thoughts

# *Living My Best Life Everyday*
## *Morning Thoughts*

Date:                                    I Feel:

I Believe Today Will Be:

I Am Grateful For:

I Woke Up Repeating To Myself:

## *Nightly Thoughts*

Time:                                    I Feel:

I Would Describe Today To Be:            Today I Started/Stopped:

My Actions Towards My Best Life          Today I Ignored/Listened To:
Were:

I Invested In:                           Today's Happiest Moment:

I Spent Time With God By:                What I Did Today That I Wanted To
                                         Do:

I Showed Love Today By:_____.

**247**

# Living My Best Life Everyday
## Morning Thoughts

Date:                                          I Feel:

I Believe Today Will Be:

I Am Grateful For:

I Woke Up Repeating To Myself:

# Nightly Thoughts

Time:                                          I Feel:

I Would Describe Today To Be:                  Today I Started/Stopped:

My Actions Towards My Best Life                Today I Ignored/Listened To:
Were:

I Invested In:                                 Today's Happiest Moment:

I Spent Time With God By:                      What I Did Today That I Wanted To
                                               Do:

I Showed Love Today By:_____.

**248**

# My Intentions Are Powerful And So Are The Actions That Follow It.

# *Living My Best Life Everyday*
## *Morning Thoughts*

Date:                                    I Feel:

I Believe Today Will Be:

I Am Grateful For:

I Woke Up Repeating To Myself:

# *Nightly Thoughts*

Time:                                    I Feel:

I Would Describe Today To Be:            Today I Started/Stopped:

My Actions Towards My Best Life          Today I Ignored/Listened To:
Were:

I Invested In:                           Today's Happiest Moment:

I Spent Time With God By:                What I Did Today That I Wanted To
                                         Do:

I Showed Love Today By:_____.

**250**

# *Living My Best Life Everyday*

## *Morning Thoughts*

Date:                                          I Feel:

I Believe Today Will Be:

I Am Grateful For:

I Woke Up Repeating To Myself:

## *Nightly Thoughts*

Time:                                          I Feel:

I Would Describe Today To Be:          Today I Started/Stopped:

My Actions Towards My Best Life       Today I Ignored/Listened To:
Were:

I Invested In:                                 Today's Happiest Moment:

I Spent Time With God By:                What I Did Today That I Wanted To
                                               Do:

I Showed Love Today By:_____.

# Living My Best Life Everyday
## Morning Thoughts

Date:                                    I Feel:

I Believe Today Will Be:

I Am Grateful For:

I Woke Up Repeating To Myself:

# Nightly Thoughts

Time:                                    I Feel:

I Would Describe Today To Be:            Today I Started/Stopped:

My Actions Towards My Best Life          Today I Ignored/Listened To:
Were:

I Invested In:                           Today's Happiest Moment:

I Spent Time With God By:                What I Did Today That I Wanted To
                                         Do:

I Showed Love Today By:_____.

# Best Life Notes & Thoughts

# *Living My Best Life Everyday*
## <u>*Morning Thoughts*</u>

Date:                                    I Feel:

I Believe Today Will Be:

I Am Grateful For:

I Woke Up Repeating To Myself:

# <u>*Nightly Thoughts*</u>

Time:                                    I Feel:

I Would Describe Today To Be:        Today I Started/Stopped:

My Actions Towards My Best Life      Today I Ignored/Listened To:
Were:

I Invested In:                       Today's Happiest Moment:

I Spent Time With God By:            What I Did Today That I Wanted To
                                     Do:

I Showed Love Today By:_____.

**254**

# *Living My Best Life Everyday*
## *Morning Thoughts*

Date:                                              I Feel:

I Believe Today Will Be:

I Am Grateful For:

I Woke Up Repeating To Myself:


# *Nightly Thoughts*

Time:                                              I Feel:

I Would Describe Today To Be:        Today I Started/Stopped:

My Actions Towards My Best Life      Today I Ignored/Listened To:
Were:

I Invested In:                               Today's Happiest Moment:

I Spent Time With God By:              What I Did Today That I Wanted To
                                              Do:

I Showed Love Today By:_____.

I Stopped Living How Everyone Thought I Should Live And Started Living A Life Filled With Purpose.